My World of Science

TRANSPARENT AND OPAQUE

Angela Royston

Heinemann Library
Chicago, Illinois

Customer Service 888-454-2279

Visit our website at www.heinemannlibrary.com

Designed by Jo Hinton-Malivoire and Tinstar Design Limited
Originated by Blenheim Colour, Ltd.
Printed and bound in China by South China Printing Company
Photo research by Maria Joannou and Sally Smith

07 06 05 04 03
10 9 8 7 6 5 4 3 2 1

Library of Congress Cataloging-in-Publication Data
Royston, Angela.
   Transparent and opaque / Angela Royston.
      v. cm. – (My world of science)
Includes bibliographical references and index.
Contents: What is transparent? – What is opaque? – What is translucent? – Shadows – Windows – Light shades – Bottles and jars – Stained glass – Making colored lights – Sunglasses – Plastic – Paper – Cloth.
   ISBN 1-40340-857-2 (HC), 1-40343-170-1 (Pbk)
   1. Transparency–Juvenile literature. 2. Opacity (Optics)–Juvenile literature. [1. Transparency. 2. Opacity (Optics)] I. Title.
   QC173.36 .R7 2003
   535'.3–dc21
                            2002009433

Acknowledgments
The author and publishers are grateful to the following for permission to reproduce copyright material:
p. 4 H. Rogers/Trip; p. 5 PhotoDisc; pp. 6, 7, 8, 10, 11, 16, 17, 21, 23, 24, 25, 26, 27, 29 Trevor Clifford;
p. 9 Rudiger Lehnen/Science Photo Library; pp. 12, 18, 22, 28 Getty Images; p. 13 L. Gullachsen/Trip;
p. 14 Ruper Horrox; p. 15 Martin Sookias; p. 19 Craig Hutchins/Eye Ubiquitous; p. 20 Network Photographers.

Cover photograph by Trevor Clifford.

Every effort has been made to contact copyright holders of any material reproduced in this book. Any omissions will be rectified in subsequent printings if notice is given to the publisher.

Some words are shown in bold, **like this.** You can find out what they mean by looking in the glossary.

Contents

What Is Transparent?

There are three **starfish** in this picture. You can even see the white starfish in the water. The water is **transparent.** You can see through it.

You see when light enters your eyes. Here you can see the food inside these glass jars. Light travels through the glass to your eyes.

What Is Opaque?

The girl cannot see what is inside the wooden box. Light does not pass through wood. It is **opaque.**

These children do not want to see each other's work. They have put an opaque **screen** between them.

What Is Translucent?

Some light passes through this glass vase. But you cannot clearly see the stems of the flowers inside. The vase is **translucent.**

This water is translucent. You can see a **sunken** ship. But the water is cloudy. You cannot see the ship clearly.

Shadows

Glass can be **transparent, translucent,** or **opaque.** The purple vase is translucent. Which vase is opaque? Which one is transparent?

Shadows are made when something blocks the light. Opaque objects make dark shadows. Transparent objects make light shadows.

Windows

Most windows are made of **transparent** glass. The glass lets you see the world outside. It also keeps out the rain and wind.

The windows in this door have **translucent** glass. They let some light in. But you cannot see through them from the outside.

Lamp Shades

Electric lightbulbs are very bright. The lamp shade is **translucent.** It only lets through some of the light from the lightbulb.

The shade on this lamp is **opaque.** Light cannot pass through it. The lightbulb only shines on the desk below. It does not bother people nearby.

Bottles and Jars

Many bottles and jars are
transparent. You can see what
is inside them. That way, you know
when the bottle or jar is almost empty.

Some bottles and jars are **opaque.**
You have to read the labels to find
out what is inside them.

Stained Glass

Some windows are made of pieces of colored glass. These are called **stained** glass windows. Sometimes the colored pieces of glass make a picture.

Clear glass lets a lot of light pass
through. The darkest pieces of glass
are the most **opaque.** Light colors
of glass are **translucent.**

Making Colored Lights

Some lightbulbs have colored glass.
These colored lightbulbs decorate the
street. The colored glass changes the
color of the light you see.

This special flashlight has red and green **screens.** It makes a green light when the green screen covers the lightbulb. The flashlight is used to make **signals.**

Sunglasses

Some sunglasses **protect** your eyes. They block out **harmful** sunlight. These harmful kinds of sunlight can hurt your eyes.

Sunglasses are **translucent.** They only let some light pass through. This makes it easier for you to see in bright sunlight.

Plastic

Plastic can be **transparent, translucent,** or **opaque.** This plastic **package** lets you see the toys. The plastic also keeps the toys clean.

Compact discs and **game cartridges** are made of plastic, too. But they are opaque. You cannot see through them.

Paper

Most kinds of paper are **opaque.**
You cannot see through this wrapping
paper. And you cannot see through the
pages of this book, either.

Tissue paper is very thin. Tissue paper is so thin that it is **translucent.** You can see some light through these tissue paper flowers.

Cloth

Most cloth is **opaque.** Many curtains are made of opaque cloth. People close their curtains at night so that streetlights do not keep them awake.

Some cloth is **translucent.** This **bride** is wearing a translucent **veil** over her face. It is difficult to see her face clearly.

Glossary

bride woman who is going to be married

compact disc circular piece of plastic that stores music

game cartridge thing that stores computer games

harmful bad for you

opaque *(oh-PAYK)* does not let any light pass through

package box or wrapping that holds something

protect keep from harm or danger

screen piece of thin material that can be opaque, colored, or translucent

shadow dark shape made when something blocks light

signal message sent by radio, light, or other method of communication

sink go below water

stain give something color

starfish star-shaped ocean animal

tissue soft, thin paper used as a handkerchief

translucent *(trans-LOO-sent)* lets some light pass through

transparent *(trans-PA-rent)* lets all light pass through

veil piece of cloth used to cover someone's face

More Books to Read

Holderness, Jackie. *What Is a Shadow?* Brookfield, Conn.: Millbrook Press, Incorporated, 2002.

Madgwick, Wendy. *Super Materials.* Austin, Tex.: Raintree Publishers, 1999.

Oxlade, Chris. *Glass.* Chicago: Heinemann Library, 2001.

Index